Praying The Our Father

Encountering God through the Ancient Tradition of Lectio Divina

Lord, teach us to pray!

Lectio Divina Catholic Prayer Journal Series

Volume 7

Katherine Mills Johnson, D.Min.

Praying The Our Father
Encountering God through the Ancient Tradition of Lectio Divina
Lectio Divina Catholic Prayer Journal Series, Volume 7

ISBN-13: 978-1494353681
ISBN-10: 1494353687

Contents

"Were not our hearts burning within us while he
was talking to us on the road, while he was
opening the scriptures to us?"

Luke 24:32

Introduction to the
Lectio Divina Catholic Prayer Journal Series

In order for us as Christians to grow in holiness and become the people we were created to be, we need to have an ongoing, experiential knowledge of the One who loves us. In one of the strongest exhortations Jesus makes to his disciples in the Upper Room discourse, he admonishes them to abide or remain in Him in the same way that a fruitful branch remains in the vine (John 15:4-10). We, just like the disciples, can do nothing without him. We must maintain that life-giving connection with the One who is indeed our Life. This is what Jesus prayed for—that we would experience and be connected to the very life and relationship that exists within the Triune God (John 17:21,23).

To develop this relationship, to grow in this journey of faith, we need to deepen our intimacy with God. At the foundational level, Christian spirituality involves encountering God, experiencing Him, and being transformed by that encounter. It embraces the use of all the means of grace that God has made available to us for cultivating and growing a deep relationship with Christ.

One of the most beautiful ways for entering into prayer is through the Word of God. Lectio divina brings you into direct conversation with the Lord and it opens for you wisdom's treasure. The intimate friendship with the One who loves us, enables us to see with the eyes of God, to speak with his Word in our hearts, to treasure the beauty of that experience and to share it with those who are hungry for eternity.
—Pope Francis

Lectio divina (literally, "sacred reading") is a way of praying that encourages this kind of intimate encounter with God. In it, we read Holy Scripture with an openness of heart, allowing it to penetrate our hearts and transform our lives though the work of the Holy Spirit. We converse with Jesus much as the disciples did on the Emmaus road when he opened the Scripture to them.

As we walk with Jesus like the disciples, or sit at his feet listening to him like Mary of Bethany, he gives us glimpses of who he is and how much he loves us. Nothing fulfills and satisfies the human heart more than seeing the beauty of the living God, listening to his voice, and being transformed in his presence. Reflecting on Scripture using *lectio divina* can be a powerful way of experiencing his presence and his transforming love in our lives.

All seven volumes in this Prayer Journal Series are intended for anyone who desires to grow in prayer and in their relationship with God. The Prayer Journals are designed to be practical, hands-on tools for praying using the ancient tradition of *lectio divina*. The introductory section in each volume gives short, easy-to-apply explanations and directions so that you can quickly begin to pray and encounter our Lord in Scripture.

The Lord's Prayer "is truly the summary of the whole gospel." "Since the Lord... after handing over the practice of prayer, said elsewhere, 'Ask and you will receive,' and since everyone has petitions which are peculiar to his circumstances, the regular and appropriate prayer [the Lord's Prayer] is said first, as the foundation of further desires." (CCC: 2761)

Praying The Our Father

The traditional expression "the Lord's Prayer"—*oratio Dominica*—means that the prayer to our Father is taught and given to us by the Lord Jesus. The prayer that comes to us from Jesus is truly unique: it is "of the Lord." On the one hand, in the words of this prayer the only Son gives us the words the Father gave him: he is the master of our prayer. On the other, as Word incarnate, he knows in his human heart the needs of his human brothers and sisters and reveals them to us: he is the model of our prayer. (CCC: 2765)

Pope Benedict XVI:

"The fact that Luke places the Our Father in the context of Jesus' own praying is...significant. Jesus thereby involves us in his own prayer; he leads us into the interior dialogue of triune love; he draws our human hardships deep into God's heart, as it were. This also means, however, that the words of the Our Father are signposts to interior prayer, they provide a basic direction for our being, and they aim to configure us to the image of the Son. The meaning of the Our Father goes much further than the mere provision of a prayer text. It aims to form our being, to train us in the inner attitude of Jesus." (Jesus of Nazareth, p. 132)

St. Cyprian on the Lord's Prayer

Let us therefore, brethren beloved, pray as God our Teacher has taught us. It is a loving and friendly prayer to beseech God with His own word, to come up to His ears in the prayer of Christ. Let the Father acknowledge the words of His Son when we make our prayer, and let Him also who dwells within in our breast Himself dwell in our voice. And since we have Him as an Advocate with the Father for our sins, let us, when as sinners we petition on behalf of our sins, put forward the words of our Advocate. For since He says, that "whatsoever we shall ask of the Father in His name, He will give us," how much more effectually do we obtain what we ask in Christ's name, if we ask for it in His own prayer! (From The Treatise on the Lord's Prayer, Ch. 3)

This *lectio divina* prayer journal is designed to be used in conjunction with praying the Our Father. It encourages anyone who desires to grow in prayer to take each of phrases of the prayer and pray with them using *lectio divina*. Scripture passages for each section of the Lord's prayer as well as inspirational quotations from the Catechism, Pope Emeritus Benedict, and the saints are included, along with instructions on the four stages of *lectio divina*. Our goal in this kind of prayer is to encounter our Lord as he speaks to our hearts and transforms our lives by the power of the Holy Spirit.

Lord, teach us to pray!

The Lord's Prayer by James Tissot

The Lord's Prayer

Our Father

who art in heaven,

hallowed be thy name.

Thy kingdom come.

Thy will be done on earth, as it is in heaven.

Give us this day our daily bread,

and forgive us our trespasses,

as we forgive those who trespass against us,

and lead us not into temptation,

but deliver us from evil.

Amen.

Matthew 6:9-13 (CCC: 2759)

A Brief Introduction to
The Ancient Tradition of Lectio Divina

A Life-giving Encounter

It is especially necessary that listening to the Word of God
should become a life-giving encounter,
in the ancient tradition of lectio divina,
which draws from the biblical text the living Word which
questions, directs and shapes our lives.

–Pope John Paul II

Why Lectio Divina?

Quotes From The Synod of Bishops on the Word of God In the Life and Mission of the Church

The Word of God is to be the primary source of inspiration in the spiritual life of the Church communities in its many practices, such as spiritual exercises, retreats, devotions and acts of piety. In this matter, an important goal (and criterion of authenticity) of this practice is to make an individual grow in a personal application of his reading of the Word for its sage teaching, its ability to help the Christian discern the realities of life and the *reasons for hope* contained therein (cf. 1 Pt 3:15), which are fundamental to Christian witness and the pursuit of holiness.

The Church's primary task is to assist the faithful in understanding how to encounter the Word of God under the guidance of the Spirit. *In a particular way*, she is to teach how this process takes place in the spiritual reading of the Bible; how the Bible, Tradition and the Magisterium are intrinsically joined by the Spirit, and what is required of the believer to be guided by the Holy Spirit received in Baptism and the other sacraments.

Above all, the Church should encourage the biblical practice traditionally called *lectio divina* with its four stages (*lectio, meditatio, oratio* and *contemplatio*). This practice was characteristic of the early days of the Church and was present throughout her history. The tradition was originally reserved to monasteries, but today the Spirit, through the Church's Magisterium, is inspiring the practise among the clergy, parish communities, ecclesial movements, families and the young.

St. Jerome observes: "The Lord's flesh is real food and his blood real drink; this is our true good in this present life: to nourish ourselves with his flesh and to drink his blood in not only the Eucharist but also the reading of Sacred Scripture. In fact, the Word of God, drawn from the knowledge of the Scriptures, is real food and real drink."

The supreme vocation of the Christian is to encounter, pray and live the Word.

What is Lectio Divina?

Since the early centuries of the church, Christians have encountered God through praying with the Holy Scriptures. *Lectio divina*, literally "sacred reading," involves reading, pondering, and praying the written Word of God so that we may encounter the living Word of God—our Lord Jesus Christ—and grow in an intimate relationship with him. Our desire is to meet God as his Word penetrates our hearts and allow him to transform us more and more into the image of Christ.

In *lectio divina*, we enter into a conversation with God. It is very different than Bible study done for the sake of gaining information about God. The aim of *lectio divina* is to nourish and deepen our relationship with God through Scripture and prayer. Through the centuries, sacred reading has been practiced in many different forms, by both groups and individuals. In his address commemorating the 40th anniversary of the Dogmatic Constitution, *Dei Verbum*, Pope Benedict XVI called upon all the faithful to renew their spiritual lives with the practice of *lectio divina*. He said,

> *I would like in particular to recall and recommend the ancient tradition of "lectio divina": the diligent reading of Sacred Scripture accompanied by prayer brings about that intimate dialogue in which the person reading hears God who is speaking, and in praying, responds to him with trusting openness of heart (c.f. Dei Verbum, n.25). If it is effectively promoted, this practice will bring to the Church - I am convinced of it - a new spiritual springtime.*

Lectio divina involves four prayer-filled stages: *lectio* (reading), *meditatio* (meditation), *oratio* (prayer) and *contemplatio* (contemplation). It is a powerful spiritual discipline for those who desire to grow in intimacy with God. In essence, *lectio divina* is prayer at a deep experiential level. It is encountering God through his Word. *Lectio divina* "...is truly capable of opening up to the faithful the treasures of God's word, but also of bringing about an encounter with Christ, the living word of God" (Pope Benedict XVI). This intimate encounter with God should lead to the genuine transformation of our lives by the power of the Holy Spirit. In this process we are also empowered to become more fruitful disciples of Jesus Christ. Some actually consider this to be a fifth stage called, *actio* (action).

Recent years have seen a great revival of interest in this ancient prayer practice. The following pages are an attempt to introduce this type of prayer in such a way that anyone who desires to try it can understand and practice this wonderful gift of the Church.

Beginning Our Prayer

Silence *"In returning and rest you shall be saved; in quietness and trust shall be your strength."* Isaiah 30:15

As we begin to pray, it is helpful to take a few moments to prepare ourselves to encounter God through his Word. Invite the presence of the Holy Spirit and acknowledge your need of him. Since sin can hinder our prayer it is also appropriate to do a short examination of conscience and ask for God's mercy (Psalm 139:23-24). When we come to God with a humble and contrite heart, he will hear us and speak to us. Also, because of our busy and noise-filled lives we need to quiet our minds and set aside the always-present "to do" list. In order to hear God's still, small voice speaking to us, it is helpful to intentionally quiet our hearts and minds, creating the inner silence we need to be able to hear. In the silence of our hearts, we turn our thoughts and attention toward God. If our desire is for God to touch our hearts and change our lives, we need to approach his word with receptivity, expectancy, and willingness to listen, change, and obey.

Shutterstock.com

The Four Stages of Lectio Divina

Read *"Speak, for your servant is listening."* 1 Samuel 3:10

The first stage of *lectio divina* is reading. If we take the time to slow down and give our full attention to God, he will speak to us through his Holy Scriptures. We begin by inviting the Holy Spirit to say to us whatever he wants us to hear. This first stage of reading the Scripture passage humbly and prayerfully is the foundation for everything else that follows. It is not reading for information as if we were preparing to teach a class or take a test; it is listening to the Word of God.

We approach reading with the knowledge that we are listening to the living Word of God. This step involves our intellect and at the same time is a prayerful and reverent act. We are deliberately and consciously making space for God and turning to him with our minds and hearts. We slowly read a short passage several times (aloud, if possible), allowing time to savor the words and let them penetrate our minds.

This is the opposite of reading quickly in order to finish a certain amount of material. Fast reading only lets the words go skin deep. In *lectio divina*, we read for depth, not breadth. The goal is to listen, *truly* listen, to the Word of God, cultivating the ability to attend deeply to what God is saying. St. Benedict called it attending "with the ear of your heart." We follow the example of Samuel, who said, "Speak, for your servant is listening" (1 Samuel 3:10). Listening to the voice of God involves being attentive to his sometimes still, small voice. Like the prophet Elijah, we may hear God, not in the earthquake or fire but in a gentle whisper (1 Kings 19:11-12).

This kind of prayerful reading runs counter to the mindset of our busy culture. The reading stage of *lectio divina* involves the freedom to read a short passage without obligation to hurriedly move on. Sometimes we actually need to give ourselves permission to take our time as we read and pray. It is helpful to remember that we are responding to a Person who desires to speak, and he may do so through a sentence, a phrase, or a single word. Our part is to quiet our hearts so that we can hear him.

We listen to the Word in the spirit of silence and awe. It is important to notice and underline or write down any words or phrases that seem to stand out. As we realize God is beginning to speak, our reading begins to move into the second stage of *lectio divina*, meditation. Each stage or movement is part of a continuously deepening prayer encounter with God.

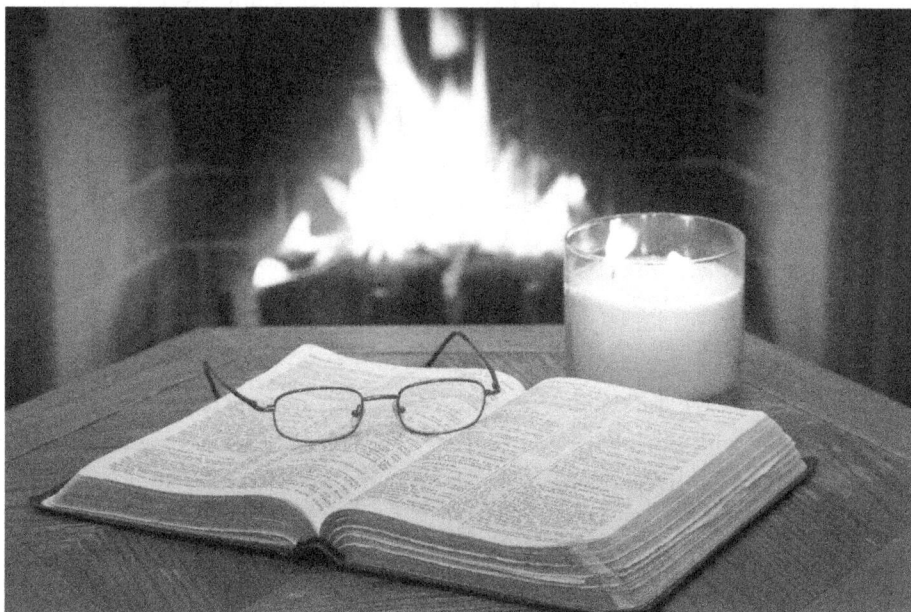

Shutterstock.com

Meditate *"Oh, how I love your law! It is my meditation all day long."* Psalm 119:97

The second stage of *lectio divina* is meditation. Reading flows into meditation as we begin to savor the truths that God is revealing. At times it is difficult to separate these two stages because they are so closely related. Fr. Jean-Pierre de Caussade shows how they intertwine, saying to read "quietly, slowly, word for word to enter into the subject more with the heart than the mind." Then he encourages pausing frequently: "From time to time make short pauses to allow these truths time to flow through all the recesses of the soul and to give occasion for the operation of the Holy Spirit who, during these peaceful pauses and times of silent attention, engraves and imprints these heavenly truths in the heart." At this point, reading and meditation are almost indistinguishable, and we should not be in a hurry.

Our model for meditation is the Blessed Virgin Mary, who pondered in her heart what she had seen and heard of Jesus (Luke 2:19). The Psalmist also knew the delights of meditation on Word of God: "Oh, how I love your law! It is my meditation all day long" (Psalm 119:97). The people of God were even commanded to meditate on the Word continually so that they would know and obey God's will for them: "This book of the law shall not depart out of your mouth; you shall meditate on it day and night, so that you may be careful to act in accordance with all that is written in it" (Joshua 1:8-9). It is a natural progression that as we read and immerse ourselves in the Word of God, we begin to think about it and consider its meaning: "I will meditate on your precepts, and fix my eyes on your ways. I will delight in your statutes; I will not forget your word" (Psalm 119:15-16).

Meditation can take the form of whatever is helpful to each individual. Some of us may use our imagination to view the passage through the eyes of the author or someone mentioned in the verses. Others of us may use a journal to help us reflect on what we have read. It is often helpful to ask a question such as "What does this mean?" As we ask, the Holy Spirit reveals to us what he wants us to know. Like the disciples on the road to Emmaus, we are able to say, "*Were not our hearts burning within us while he was talking to us on the road, while he was opening the scriptures to us*" (Luke 24:32)?

In *lectio divina*, we seek to know the mind of Christ and his will for our lives. The Word often acts as a mirror for us when God shows us something in our lives he wants to change. "The meditator ponders and perceives the hidden lessons in the Word of God in such a way that wisdom for life is learned," writes Carmelite S. A. Morello. We approach the Scripture with faith, expecting God to speak. The constant factor, no matter what means are used, is that we are drawn to God in some way during this process of prayerful reflection.

This practice of meditation is a crucial aspect of our life of faith. The Word of God transforms and renews our minds and gives us a firm foundation for our lives. We learn about God—who he is and how he works in the world and in our lives. We also learn the truth about ourselves—our purpose and significance in creation and in life. Our prayer experience, however, must not remain solely on this intellectual level. Our goal is more than just knowledge about God. It is knowing God himself. In *lectio divina*, this begins to occur as we move from reflecting with our minds to responding in prayer with our hearts.

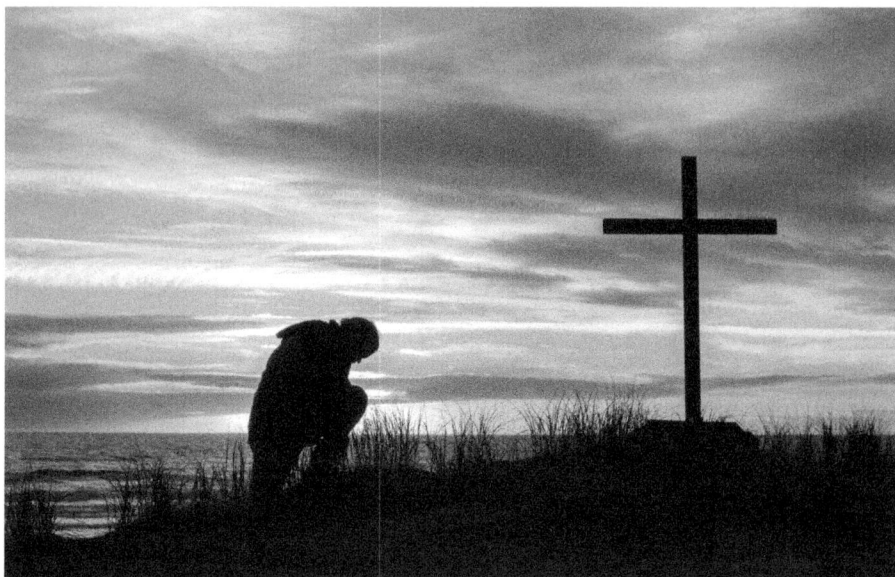

Pray *"I call upon you, for you will answer me, O God...."* Psalm 17:6

> *Fundamentally, it is the atmosphere of prayer that penetrates every aspect of holy reading that makes it distinctive. Prayer is not suddenly born at the third stage. Rather, prayer accompanies us as we open the book and settle our mind, as we read the page and ponder its meaning. Prayer is the meaning of lectio divina; that is why the exercise of sacred reading is sometimes said to be a technique of prayer.*
> —Fr. Michael Casey, OSCO

The third stage of *lectio divina* is prayer. It follows naturally that we move from meditation into prayer. As with reading and meditation, it can be difficult to determine when meditation ends and prayer begins. As we ponder a Scripture passage and think about what it means, spontaneous prayers of thanks, repentance, or intercession may arise from our hearts. We may also ask the Lord how he wants us to apply the truth of his Word to our specific life situation.

At a certain point, our prayer moves from being centered in the intellect to being prayer from the heart. Prayer happens as the living Word touches our hearts and we respond to him at a deep inner level. Thelma Hall says, "[Prayer] is the unique and spontaneous voice of the heart which is touched by God and reaches out to him in ardent love." Prayer with Scripture helps draw us into a deeper encounter with the living God through his Word.

Listening is an integral part of prayer. We move from meditation to prayer as we, with open hearts, make ourselves available to the Spirit of God so that he is speaking and we are listening. Many times we think that prayer is supposed to be us talking and asking for things while God listens. In *lectio divina*, we learn to listen and to be comfortable with silence. Take time to wait for him to respond to your prayer and speak to your heart. We can be confident that God will speak to our hearts as we quiet ourselves before him. "I call upon you, for you will answer me, O God; incline your ear to me, hear my words." (Psalm 17:6). Many times he is just waiting for us to open ourselves to hear him and to give him time to commune with us.

> *Let us now remain silent, to hear the word of God with effectiveness and let us*
> *maintain this silence after hearing, so that it may continue to dwell in us, to*
> *live in us, and to speak to us. Let it resonate at the beginning of our day so*
> *that God has the first word and let it echo in us in the evening so that God*
> *has the last word.* –Pope Benedict XVI

In prayer, we experience the same longing and desire for God himself that the Psalmist expresses, "As a deer longs for flowing streams, so my soul longs for you, O God. My soul thirsts for God, for the living God" (Psalm 42:1-2). This increase of desire for God is awakened in prayer as we encounter him in intimate conversation, inviting him to do his work in our hearts. The realization of weakness and sinfulness drives us to an even deeper longing for him and his purifying love and grace. Prayer is a humble seeking and desiring after what God has revealed through his Word. It is the soul calling out with longing for that which it cannot attain on its own.

Contemplate *"Be still and know that I am God."* Psalm 46:10

> *Contemplation is nothing else than a secret and peaceful and loving inflow of*
> *God, which, if not hampered, fires the soul in the spirit of love.*
> —St. John of the Cross

The fourth stage and ultimate goal of *lectio divina* is contemplation. This stage of prayer gives us the opportunity for an intimate time of communion with the Lord. Contemplation is simply a loving awareness of God in which he pours his love into our hearts. It is finding ourselves in the presence of Jesus. St. John of the Cross calls it the "divine inflow." It has also been described as "resting in

God" or a "loving gaze" upon him. Contemplation is a gift from God that enables us to rest in his presence and enter his loving and transforming embrace. God himself calls us into this silence of heart: "Be still, and know that I am God" (Psalm 46:10). David longed for times of being in the presence of God and gazing upon his beauty (Psalm 27:4). Jesus went frequently to be alone with his Father.

There are times in all loving relationships when words are not necessary. In this stage we stop speaking and, in silence, simply enjoy being in the presence of God. He speaks to us or is present with us in ways that, like the title of a book by Thelma Hall, is "too deep for words." This is a place where deep transformation of our hearts and lives occurs. Just take time to be with him and let him love you and refresh your soul. M. Gildas' analysis of the words of Bernard of Clairvaux helps us gain additional insight into this stage of prayer:

> According to St. Bernard (De Consider., lib. I, c. vii) this is the highest form of human worship, as it is essentially an act of adoration and of utter self-surrender of man's whole being....It is a soul lost in admiration and love of the Eternal Beauty, the sight of which though but a feeble reflection, fill it with a joy naught else in the world can give – a joy which, far more eloquently than speech, testifies that the soul rates that Beauty above all other beauties, and finds in It the completion of all its desires.

Contemplation is prayer that we do not control or achieve; it is an encounter initiated by God himself and leads to union with him. Contemplative awareness of God is a pure gift from God and not a result of anything we do. It is a spiritual experience and a process of interior transformation. Anyone can experience resting silently in God's loving presence, provided they open their heart and mind to God. All prayer should lead to a life-changing encounter with God. At times we will be aware of this transforming work of the Holy Spirit in our hearts. At other

times it is a matter of faith and trust that God is with us and transforming us according to his promises.

This stage of *lectio divina* is not a mysterious method of prayer reserved for an elite few. Basil Pennington states, "All those who regularly meet the Lord in lectio will go beyond all the thoughts and ideas and concepts, no matter how fascinating they are, and enter into a contemplative union with God in Christ. They will come to have the mind and heart of Christ." Here, as we rest in God, he satisfies the ultimate longing, thirst and need of the human soul. It is in God himself that hearts are satisfied. St. Augustine said, "...you have made us for yourself, and our heart is restless till it finds its rest in you."

> *The Lord...does not wait until the longing soul has said all its say, but breaks in upon the middle of its prayer, runs to meet it in all haste, sprinkled with sweet heavenly dew, anointed with the most precious perfumes, and He restores the weary soul, He slakes its thirst, He feeds its hunger, He makes the soul forget all earthly things: by making it die to itself He gives it new life in a wonderful way, and by making it drunk He brings it back to its true senses.*
>
> —Guigo II (1140-1193), Carthusian Monk

~ ~ ~ ~ ~ ~ ~

Although we have divided the stages of lectio divina and discussed each one separately, it is also important to point out that these are movements along a continuum of prayer. At different times we may experience some or all of the stages and not necessarily in the order described.

Ending Our Prayer

Action "My Father is glorified by this, that you bear much fruit...." John 15:8

One of the results of encountering the Lord in prayer is that our lives are changed and we become more like Christ. As we draw close to him and his Word transforms our hearts, we will begin to live more and more like a fruitful disciple of Jesus. Our desire to obey him will grow stronger as we spend time with him. "The process of *lectio divina* is not concluded until it arrives at action ('actio'), which moves the believer to make his or her life a gift for others in charity" (Pope Benedict XVI). This is why at the end of our prayer time we ask "How is God calling me to act in response to what he has shown me?"

Helpful Suggestions for Prayer

Place and Time

Set aside a place to pray that is as free of distractions as possible. A quiet room in your home, a park bench, or the adoration chapel at church may provide just the kind of place you need. Choose a time that works best for you. For many, morning is best because prayer is a wonderful way to consecrate ourselves to the Lord and commit our day to him.

A Humble Heart

It is important to examine ourselves and humble ourselves before God as we come to our time of prayer. "God opposes the proud, but gives grace to the humble" (James 4:6). When we come to God with a humble and contrite heart, he will hear us and speak to us.

Barriers

Various things can hinder our prayers. Some involve sins, such as pride, laziness, unforgiveness, hardness of heart, etc. Before you begin your prayer, take time to ask God to give you a soft heart that is open, ready to listen, and able to receive God's gifts. If any sins come to mind, acknowledge them and resolve to amend your life with God's help. Call upon the Holy Spirit, for without him, *lectio divina* is just human effort or an intellectual activity. Distractions are another hindrance to prayer. If you are bothered by thoughts of what you need to do that day, simply make a list of them and then return to the list after your prayer time.

Shutterstock.com

Lectio Divina Summary

Begin with Silence

1. **Reading** – Read the passage through slowly and attentively several times (out loud if possible), savoring the words and letting them sink in. Write down any words or phrases that seem to stand out.

2. **Meditation** – Now begin to think about the words or phrases that stood out to you. Come in faith with the expectation that the Lord will speak to you. Ask him a question such as "What does this mean?" to help you reflect more deeply. You may also think about the passage through the eyes of the author or someone mentioned in the verses. Write down any insights that God gives you .

3. **Prayer** – Prayer is a two-way conversation with the Lord. Respond from your heart to what he has been revealing to you in his Word, especially taking time to listen to what he may be saying to you personally. You may want to write out your prayer to God and anything he says to you.

4. **Contemplation** – At any time, when you begin to sense the presence of the Lord, stop any mental effort you are making and just rest in and enjoy his presence. This is the time to savor the special moment of connection between you and God. Treasure God's Word in your heart, and like Mary respond, "I am your servant. Be it done unto me according to your word" (Luke 1:38). Remember that contemplation is a gift from God and not something we can do ourselves.

End with Action

Read

"Speak, for your servant is listening."
1 Samuel 3:10

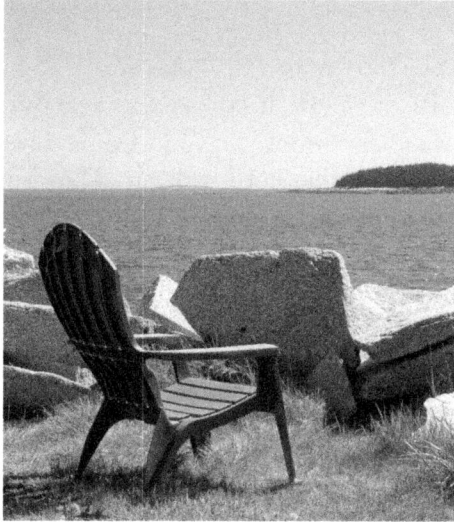

Contemplate

"Be still and know that I am God."
Psalm 46:10

Meditate

"Oh, how I love your law! It is my meditation all day long."
Psalm 119:97

Pray

"I call upon you, for you will answer me, O God...."
Psalm 17:6

How to Use This Prayer Journal

As you begin to use the journal pages of this prayer guide, read the Scripture verses at the top of the page and then follow the four stages of Read, Meditate, Pray, and Contemplate. Write down what God is showing you on the journal pages provided. A synopsis of the stages can be found under each verse. You can also refer back to the introduction or the summary on page 23 at any time for a more detailed description of the stages.

A unique feature of this Prayer Journal is the included quotations from saints as well as from the Catechism of the Catholic Church. These are interspersed throughout the journal pages to give added insight to your reflection and prayer. A brief quote from Pope Emeritus Benedict's book, *Jesus of Nazareth*, introduces each section of the Prayer Journal.

It is important to write down your thoughts and prayers as God leads you. Remember that the outline of the stages is there to help and is not a hard and fast rule to be followed exactly in order. You may find yourself from time to time going back and forth between the stages. The important thing is that this is a time of prayer and communion with our Lord.

We know that the Word of God is always fresh and life-giving. One special thing about this prayer journal is that it can be used multiple times. If you come back to a particular passage you can continue writing in the journal or use extra paper or a notebook to record what God is showing you. It can be encouraging to look back at what you have written and see how God has been speaking to you and transforming your life.

O Lord, today I

Praying
The Our Father

Prayer Journal

German text of the Our Father with the Trinity in central column and scenes depicting the parts of the prayer in side columns. Author unknown.

Our Father

We begin with the salutation "Father." Reinhold Schneider writes of this in his exposition of the Our Father: "The Our Father begins with a great consolation: we are allowed to say 'Father.' This one word contains the whole history of redemption. We are allowed to say 'Father,' because the Son was our brother and has revealed the Father to us; because, thanks to what Christ has done, we have once more become children of God." It is true, of course, that contemporary men and women have difficulty experiencing the great consolation of the word father immediately, since the experience of the father is in many cases either completely absent or is obscured by inadequate examples of fatherhood.

We must therefore let Jesus teach us what father really means. In Jesus' discourses, the Father appears as the source of all good, as the measure of the rectitude (perfection) of man. The love that endures "to the end" (Jn 13:1), which the Lord fulfilled on the Cross in praying for his enemies, shows us the essence of the Father. He is this love. Because Jesus brings it to completion, he is entirely "Son," and he invites us to become "sons" according to this criterion.

From *Jesus of Nazareth* by Pope Benedict XVI, p. 135-6.

Our Father

But whenever you pray, go into your room and shut the door and pray to your Father who is in secret; and your Father who sees in secret will reward you. *Matthew 6:6*

But to all who received him, who believed in his name, he gave power to become children of God, who were born, not of blood or of the will of the flesh or of the will of man, but of God. *John 1:12-13*

But when the fullness of time had come, God sent his Son, born of a woman, born under the law, in order to redeem those who were under the law, so that we might receive adoption as children. And because you are children, God has sent the Spirit of his Son into our hearts, crying, "Abba! Father!" So you are no longer a slave but a child, and if a child then also an heir, through God. *Galatians 4:6*

---

1. *Read* – Read the verses slowly and prayerfully several times (out loud if possible), savoring the words and letting them sink in. Write down any words or phrases that seem to stand out:

2. *Meditate* – Now begin to think about the words or phrases that stood out to you. Come in faith with the expectation that the Lord will speak to you. Ask him a question such as "What does this mean?" to help you reflect more deeply. You may also think about the passage through the eyes of the author or someone mentioned in the verses. Write down any insights that God gives you:

3. *Pray* – Prayer is a two-way conversation with the Lord. Respond from your heart to what he has been revealing to you in his Word, especially taking time to listen to what he may be saying to you personally. You may want to write out your prayer to God and anything he says to you:

4. *Contemplate* – At any time, when you begin to sense the presence of the Lord, stop any mental effort you are making and just rest in and enjoy his presence.

From the Catechism

The baptized cannot pray to "our" Father without bringing before him all those for whom he gave his beloved Son. God's love has no bounds, neither should our prayer. Praying "our" Father opens to us the dimensions of his love revealed in Christ: praying with and for all who do not yet know him, so that Christ may "gather into one the children of God." (CCC: 2793)

Journal Page

From Pope Benedict XVI

"The word 'our' is really rather demanding. It requires that we step out of the closed circle of our 'I'. It requires that we surrender ourselves to communion with the other children of God. It requires, then, that we strip ourselves of what is merely our own, of what divides. It requires that we accept the other, the others – that we open our ear and our heart to them. When we say the word 'our', we say 'yes' to the living Church in which the Lord wanted to gather his new family. In this sense, the Our Father is at once a fully personal and thoroughly ecclesial prayer. (*Jesus of Nazareth, p. 141*)

From the Catechism

The first phrase of the Our Father is a blessing of adoration before it is a supplication. For it is the glory of God that we should recognize him as "Father," the true God. We give him thanks for having revealed his name to us, for the gift of believing in it, and for the indwelling of his Presence in us. (CCC: 2781)

Contemplate Meditate Pray Read Contemplate Meditate Pray Read Contemplate Meditate Pray Read

From St. Cyprian

The new man, born again and restored to his God by His grace, says "Father," in the first place, because he has now begun to be a son. (*Treatise on the Lord's Prayer*, Ch 9)

From Pope Benedict XVI

We are not ready-made children of God from the start, but we are meant to become so increasingly by growing more and more deeply in communion with Jesus. Our sonship turns out to be identical with following Christ. To name God as Father thus becomes a summons to us: to live as a 'child', as a son or daughter. 'All that is mine is thine,' Jesus says in his high-priestly prayer to the Father (Jn 17:10), and the father says the same thing to the elder brother of the prodigal son (Lk 15:31). The word *father* is an invitation to live from our awareness of this reality. (*Jesus of Nazareth*, p. 138)

From St. Augustine

Our Father: at this name love is aroused in us...and the confidence of obtaining what we are about to ask.... What would he not give to his children who ask, since he has already granted them the gift of being his children? (CCC: 2785)

~~~~~~~~~~

How is God calling you to act in response to what he has shown you?

Who Art in Heaven

With these words, we are not pushing God the Father away to some distant planet. Rather, we are testifying to the fact that, while we have different earthly fathers, we all come from one single Father, who is the measure and source of all fatherhood. As Saint Paul says: "I bow my knees before the Father, from whom every fatherhood in heaven and on earth is named" (Eph 3:14-15).

God's fatherhood is more real than human fatherhood, because he is the ultimate source of our being; because he gives us our true paternal home, which is eternal. And if earthly fatherhood divides, heavenly fatherhood unites. Heaven, then, means that other divine summit from which we all come and to which we are all meant to return. The fatherhood that is "in heaven" points us toward the greater "we" that transcends all boundaries, breaks down all walls, and creates peace.

From *Jesus of Nazareth* by Pope Benedict XVI, p. 141-2.

Who Art In Heaven

Yet the Most High does not dwell in houses made with human hands; as the prophet says, 'Heaven is my throne, and the earth is my footstool. What kind of house will you build for me, says the Lord, or what is the place of my rest?' *Acts 7:48-49*

But God, who is rich in mercy, out of the great love with which he loved us even when we were dead through our trespasses, made us alive together with Christ—by grace you have been saved—and raised us up with him and seated us with him in the heavenly places in Christ Jesus, *Ephesians 2:4-6*

Whom have I in heaven but you? And there is nothing on earth that I desire other than you. *Psalm 73:25*

So if you have been raised with Christ, seek the things that are above, where Christ is, seated at the right hand of God. Set your minds on things that are above, not on things that are on earth, for you have died, and your life is hidden with Christ in God. *Colossians 3:1-3*

---

1. *Read* — Read the verses slowly and prayerfully several times (out loud if possible), savoring the words and letting them sink in. Write down any words or phrases that seem to stand out:

2. *Meditate* – Now begin to think about the words or phrases that stood out to you. Come in faith with the expectation that the Lord will speak to you. Ask him a question such as "What does this mean?" to help you reflect more deeply. You may also think about the passage through the eyes of the author or someone mentioned in the verses. Write down any insights that God gives you:

3. *Pray* – Prayer is a two-way conversation with the Lord. Respond from your heart to what he has been revealing to you in his Word, especially taking time to listen to what he may be saying to you personally. You may want to write out your prayer to God and anything he says to you:

4. *Contemplate* — At any time, when you begin to sense the presence of the Lord, stop any mental effort you are making and just rest in and enjoy his presence.

From the Catechism

The symbol of the heavens refers us back to the mystery of the covenant we are living when we pray to our Father. He is in heaven, his dwelling place; the Father's house is our homeland. Sin has exiled us from the land of the covenant, but conversion of heart enables us to return to the Father, to heaven. In Christ, then, heaven and earth are reconciled, for the Son alone "descended from heaven" and causes us to ascend there with him, by his Cross, Resurrection, and Ascension. (CCC: 2795)

Journal Page

From the Catechism

"Who art in heaven" does not refer to a place but to God's majesty and his presence in the hearts of the just. Heaven, the Father's house, is the true homeland toward which we are heading and to which, already, we belong. (CCC: 2802)

Contemplate Meditate Pray Read Contemplate Meditate Pray Read Contemplate Meditate Pray Read

From St. John Chrysostom
When He says, "...in heaven," He says this not to limit God to the heavens, but to withdraw from the earth the one who is in prayer, and to fix him in the high places and in the dwellings above.
(*Homily 19 on Matthew*, 6)

Contemplate Meditate Pray Read Contemplate Meditate Pray Read Contemplate Meditate Pray Read Contemplate Meditate Pray Read

From St. Cyprian

Moreover, in His teaching the Lord has bidden us to pray in secret—in hidden and remote places, in our very bed-chambers—which is best suited to faith, that we may know that God is everywhere present, and hears and sees all, and in the plenitude of His majesty penetrates even into hidden and secret places, as it is written, "I am a God at hand, and not a God afar off. If a man shall hide himself in secret places, shall I not then see him? Do not I fill heaven and earth?" (*Treatise on the Lord's Prayer*, Ch 4)

From the Catechism

When the Church prays "our Father who art in heaven," she is professing that we are the People of God, already seated "with him in the heavenly places in Christ Jesus" and "hidden with Christ in God;" yet at the same time, "here indeed we groan, and long to put on our heavenly dwelling." (CCC: 2796)

~~~~~~~~~

How is God calling you to act in response to what he has shown you?

Shutterstock.com

Hallowed Be Thy Name

...God establishes a relationship between himself and us. He puts himself within reach of our invocation. He enters into relationship with us and enables us to be in relationship with him. Yet this means that in some sense he hands himself over to our human world. He has made himself accessible and, therefore, vulnerable as well. He assumes the risk of relationship, of communion with us.

This enables us to understand what the petition for the sanctification of the divine name means. The name of God can now be misused and so God himself can be sullied.

How do I treat God's holy name? Do I stand in reverence before the mystery of the burning bush, before his incomprehensible closeness, even to the point of his presence in the Eucharist, where he truly gives himself entirely into our hands? Do I take care that God's holy companionship with us will draw us up into his purity and sanctity, instead of dragging him down into the filth?

From *Jesus of Nazareth* by Pope Benedict XVI, p. 142-145.

Hallowed Be Thy Name

I give you thanks, O Lord, with my whole heart; before the gods I sing your praise; I bow down toward your holy temple and give thanks to your name for your steadfast love and your faithfulness; for you have exalted your name and your word above everything. *Psalm 138:1-2*

Like obedient children, do not be conformed to the desires that you formerly had in ignorance. Instead, as he who called you is holy, be holy yourselves in all your conduct; for it is written, "You shall be holy, for I am holy." *1 Peter 1:14-16*

...let your light shine before others, so that they may see your good works and give glory to your Father in heaven. *Matthew 5:16*

And the four living creatures, each of them with six wings, are full of eyes all around and inside. Day and night without ceasing they sing, "Holy, holy, holy, the Lord God the Almighty, who was and is and is to come." *Revelation 4:8*

---

1. ***Read*** — Read the verses slowly and prayerfully several times (out loud if possible), savoring the words and letting them sink in. Write down any words or phrases that seem to stand out:

2. ***Meditate*** – Now begin to think about the words or phrases that stood out to you. Come in faith with the expectation that the Lord will speak to you. Ask him a question such as "What does this mean?" to help you reflect more deeply. You may also think about the passage through the eyes of the author or someone mentioned in the verses. Write down any insights that God gives you:

3. ***Pray*** – Prayer is a two-way conversation with the Lord. Respond from your heart to what he has been revealing to you in his Word, especially taking time to listen to what he may be saying to you personally. You may want to write out your prayer to God and anything he says to you:

4. ***Contemplate*** — At any time, when you begin to sense the presence of the Lord, stop any mental effort you are making and just rest in and enjoy his presence.

From St. John Chrysostom
It is worthy of him who calls God "Father" to ask nothing before the glory of His Father and to account all things secondary to the work of praising Him. "Hallowed" means glorified. God's own glory is complete and ever continues the same, but He commands him who prays to seek that He may be glorified also by our lives. (*Homily 19 on Matthew*, 7)

Journal Page

Read Pray Meditate Contemplate Read Pray Meditate Contemplate Read Pray Meditate Contemplate Read Pray Meditate Contemplate

From the Catechism

Asking the Father that his name be made holy draws us into his plan of loving kindness for the fullness of time, "according to his purpose which he set forth in Christ," that we might "be holy and blameless before him in love." (CCC: 2807)

From St. Cyprian

After this we say, "Hallowed be Thy name;" not that we wish for God that He may be hallowed by our prayers, but that we beseech of Him that His name may be hallowed in us...that we who were sanctified in baptism may continue in that which we have begun to be. (*Treatise on the Lord's Prayer*, Ch. 12)

Journal Page

Read Pray Meditate Contemplate Read Pray Meditate Contemplate Read Pray Meditate Contemplate

From the Catechism

In Jesus the name of the Holy God is revealed and given to us, in the flesh, as Savior, revealed by what he is, by his word, and by his sacrifice. This is the heart of his priestly prayer: "Holy Father...for their sake I consecrate my self, that they also may be consecrated in truth." (CCC: 2812)

From St. Peter Chrysologus

We ask God to hallow his name, which by its own holiness saves and makes holy all creation....It is this name that gives salvation to a lost world. But we ask that this name of God should be hallowed in us through our actions. For God's name is blessed when we live well, but is blasphemed when we live wickedly....We ask then that, just as the name of God is holy, so we may obtain his holiness in our souls. (CCC: 2814)

Journal Page

~~~~~~~~~

How is God calling you to act in response to what he has shown you?

Thy Kingdom Come

With the petition "thy Kingdom come" (not "our kingdom"), the Lord wants to show us how to pray and order our action in just this way. The first and essential thing is a listening heart, so that God, not we, may reign. The Kingdom of God comes by way of a listening heart. That is its path. And that is what we must pray for again and again.

To pray for the Kingdom of God is to say to Jesus: Let us be yours, Lord! Pervade us, live in us; gather scattered humanity in your body, so that in you everything may be subordinated to God and you can then hand over the universe to the Father, in order that "God may be all in all" (1 Cor 15:28).

From *Jesus of Nazareth* by Pope Benedict XVI, p. 146-147.

Thy Kingdom Come

The Lord has established his throne in the heavens, and his kingdom rules over all. *Psalm 103:19*

Once Jesus was asked by the Pharisees when the kingdom of God was coming, and he answered, "The kingdom of God is not coming with things that can be observed; nor will they say, 'Look, here it is!' or 'There it is!' For, in fact, the kingdom of God is among you." *Luke 17:20-21*

Then Jesus went about all the cities and villages, teaching in their synagogues, and proclaiming the good news of the kingdom, and curing every disease and every sickness. *Matthew 9:35*

Jesus answered..."Again, the kingdom of heaven is like a merchant in search of fine pearls; on finding one pearl of great value, he went and sold all that he had and bought it. *Matthew 13:45-46*

For the kingdom of God is not food and drink but righteousness and peace and joy in the Holy Spirit. *Romans 14:17*

---

1. ***Read*** – Read the verses slowly and prayerfully several times (out loud if possible), savoring the words and letting them sink in. Write down any words or phrases that seem to stand out:

2. ***Meditate*** - Now begin to think about the words or phrases that stood out to you. Come in faith with the expectation that the Lord will speak to you. Ask him a question such as "What does this mean?" to help you reflect more deeply. You may also think about the passage through the eyes of the author or someone mentioned in the verses. Write down any insights that God gives you:

3. ***Pray*** - Prayer is a two-way conversation with the Lord. Respond from your heart to what he has been revealing to you in his Word, especially taking time to listen to what he may be saying to you personally. You may want to write out your prayer to God and anything he says to you:

4. ***Contemplate*** – At any time, when you begin to sense the presence of the Lord, stop any mental effort you are making and just rest in and enjoy his presence.

From the Catechism

The Kingdom of God lies ahead of us. It is brought near in the Word incarnate, it is proclaimed throughout the whole Gospel, and it has come in Christ's death and Resurrection. The Kingdom of God has been coming since the Last Supper and, in the Eucharist, it is in our midst. The kingdom will come in glory when Christ hands it over to his Father. (CCC: 2816)

Read Pray Meditate Contemplate Read Pray Meditate Contemplate Read Pray Meditate Contemplate

From St. Augustine

"Come," is to be understood in the sense of "be manifested to men." For in the same way that a light which is present is absent to the blind and to those who shut their eyes, so the Kingdom of God, though it never departs from the earth, is yet absent to those who are ignorant of it. (*Our Lord's Sermon on the Mount,* Book 1 Ch. 16:20)

From the Catechism

By his word, through signs that manifest the reign of God, and by sending out his disciples, Jesus calls all people to come together around him. But above all in the great Paschal mystery—his death on the cross and his Resurrection —he would accomplish the coming of his kingdom. "And I, when I am lifted up from the earth, will draw all men to myself." Into this union with Christ all men are called. (CCC: 542)

From St. Cyprian

Christ Himself, dearest brethren, however, may be the kingdom of God, whom we day by day desire to come, whose advent we crave to be quickly manifested to us. For since He is Himself the Resurrection, since in Him we rise again, so also the kingdom of God may be understood to be Himself, since in Him we shall reign... And therefore he who dedicates himself to God and Christ, desires not earthly, but heavenly kingdoms. (*Treatise on the Lord's Prayer*, Ch. 13)

~~~~~~~~~~

How is God calling you to act in response to what he has shown you?

The Agony in the Garden
"Not my will but yours be done"

Thy Will Be Done,
On Earth As It Is In Heaven

When Jesus speaks to us of God's will and of heaven, the place where God's will is fulfilled, the core of what he says is again connected with his mission. At Jacob's well, he says to the disciples who bring him food: "My food is to do the will of him who sent me, and to accomplish his work" (Jn 4:34). What he means is that his oneness with the Father's will is the foundation of his life. The unity of his will with the Father's will is the core of his very being. ...We now understand that Jesus himself is "heaven" in the deepest and truest sense of the word—he in whom and through whom God's will is wholly done.

What we are ultimately praying for in this third petition of the Our Father is that we come closer and closer to him, so that God's will can conquer the downward pull of our selfishness and make us capable of the lofty height to which we are called.

From *Jesus of Nazareth* by Pope Benedict XVI, p. 149-150.

Thy Will Be Done On Earth As It Is In Heaven

I appeal to you therefore, brothers and sisters, by the mercies of God, to present your bodies as a living sacrifice, holy and acceptable to God, which is your spiritual worship. Do not be conformed to this world, but be transformed by the renewing of your minds, so that you may discern what is the will of God—what is good and acceptable and perfect. *Romans 12:1-2*

And going a little farther, he [Jesus] threw himself on the ground and prayed, "My Father, if it is possible, let this cup pass from me; yet not what I want but what you want." *Matthew 26:39*

Do not love the world or the things in the world. The love of the Father is not in those who love the world; for all that is in the world—the desire of the flesh, the desire of the eyes, the pride in riches—comes not from the Father but from the world. And the world and its desire are passing away, but those who do the will of God live forever. *1 John 2:15-17*

Then Mary said, "Here am I, the servant of the Lord; let it be with me according to your word." *Luke 1:38*

---

1. ***Read*** — Read the verses slowly and prayerfully several times (out loud if possible), savoring the words and letting them sink in. Write down any words or phrases that seem to stand out:

2. ***Meditate*** – Now begin to think about the words or phrases that stood out to you. Come in faith with the expectation that the Lord will speak to you. Ask him a question such as "What does this mean?" to help you reflect more deeply. You may also think about the passage through the eyes of the author or someone mentioned in the verses. Write down any insights that God gives you:

3. ***Pray*** – Prayer is a two-way conversation with the Lord. Respond from your heart to what he has been revealing to you in his Word, especially taking time to listen to what he may be saying to you personally. You may want to write out your prayer to God and anything he says to you:

4. ***Contemplate*** — At any time, when you begin to sense the presence of the Lord, stop any mental effort you are making and just rest in and enjoy his presence.

Journal Page

From the Catechism

The prayer of faith consists not only in saying "Lord, Lord," but in disposing the heart to do the will of the Father. Jesus calls his disciples to bring into their prayer this concern for cooperating with the divine plan. (CCC: 2611)

Journal Page

From the Catechism

We ask our Father to unite our will to his Son's, in order to fulfill his will, his plan of salvation for the life of the world. We are radically incapable of this, but united with Jesus and with the power of his Holy Spirit, we can surrender our will to him and decide to choose what his Son has always chosen: to do what is pleasing to the Father. (CCC: 2825)

From St. Cyprian

For since we possess the body from the earth and the spirit from heaven, we ourselves are earth and heaven; and in both we pray that God's will may be done. For between the flesh and spirit there is a struggle; and there is a daily strife as they disagree one with the other, so that we cannot do those very things that we would, in that the spirit seeks heavenly and divine things, while the flesh lusts after earthly and temporal things; and therefore we ask that, by the help and assistance of God, agreement may be made between these two natures, so that while the will of God is done both in the spirit and in the flesh, the soul which is new-born by Him may be preserved. (*Treatise on the Lord's Prayer*, Ch 16)

Read Pray Meditate Contemplate Read Pray Meditate Contemplate Read Pray Meditate Contemplate Read Pray Meditate Contemplate

From St. Cyprian

But since we are hindered by the devil from obeying with our thought and deed God's will in all things, we pray and ask that God's will may be done in us; and that it may be done in us we have need of God's good will, that is, of His help and protection, since no one is strong in his own strength, but he is safe by the grace and mercy of God. (*Treatise on the Lord's Prayer* Ch 14)

From the Catechism

Our Father "desires all men to be saved and to come to the knowledge of the truth." He "is forbearing toward you, not wishing that any should perish." His commandment is "that you love one another; even as I have loved you, that you also love one another." This commandment summarizes all the others and expresses his entire will. (CCC: 2822)

From the Catechism

"If any one is a worshiper of God and does his will, God listens to him." Such is the power of the Church's prayer in the name of her Lord, above all in the Eucharist. Her prayer is also a communion of intercession with the all-holy Mother of God and all the saints who have been pleasing to the Lord because they willed his will alone. (CCC: 2827)

~~~~~~~~~

How is God calling you to act in response to what he has shown you?

Give Us This Day Our Daily Bread

The fourth petition of the Our Father appears to us as the most "human" of all the petitions: Though the Lord directs our eyes to the essential, to the "one thing necessary," he also knows about and acknowledges our earthly needs. While he says to his disciples, "Do not be anxious about your life, what you shall eat" (Mt 6:25), he nevertheless invites us to pray for our food and thus to turn our care over to God. ...We have the right and the duty to ask for what we need. We know that if even earthly fathers give their children good things when they ask for them, God will not refuse us the good things that he alone can give (cf. Lk 11:9-13).

The great discourse on the bread of life in John 6 discloses the full spectrum of meaning of this theme. It begins with the hunger of the people who have been listening to Jesus and whom he does not send away without food, that is to say, the "necessary bread" that we require in order to live.

But Jesus does not allow us to stop there and reduce man's needs to bread, to biological and material necessities. "Man shall not live by bread alone, but by every word that proceeds from the mouth of God" (Mt 4:4; Deut 8:3). The miraculously multiplied bread harks back to the miracle of manna in the desert and at the same time points beyond itself: to the fact that man's real food is the Logos, the eternal Word, the eternal meaning, from which we come and toward which our life is directed.

The incarnate Lord gives himself to us in the Sacrament, and in that way the eternal Word for the first time becomes fully manna, the gift of the bread of the future given to us already today.

From *Jesus of Nazareth* by Pope Benedict XVI, p. 150-155.

Give Us This Day Our Daily Bread

Therefore do not worry, saying, 'What will we eat?' or 'What will we drink?' or 'What will we wear?' For it is the Gentiles who strive for all these things; and indeed your heavenly Father knows that you need all these things. But strive first for the kingdom of God and his righteousness, and all these things will be given to you as well. *Matthew 6:31-33*

I am the living bread that came down from heaven. Whoever eats of this bread will live forever; and the bread that I will give for the life of the world is my flesh. The Jews then disputed among themselves, saying, "How can this man give us his flesh to eat?" So Jesus said to them, "Very truly, I tell you, unless you eat the flesh of the Son of Man and drink his blood, you have no life in you. Those who eat my flesh and drink my blood have eternal life, and I will raise them up on the last day; for my flesh is true food and my blood is true drink." *John 6:51-55*

1. *Read* — Read the verses slowly and prayerfully several times (out loud if possible), savoring the words and letting them sink in. Write down any words or phrases that seem to stand out:

2. *Meditate* - Now begin to think about the words or phrases that stood out to you. Come in faith with the expectation that the Lord will speak to you. Ask him a question such as "What does this mean?" to help you reflect more deeply. You may also think about the passage through the eyes of the author or someone mentioned in the verses. Write down any insights that God gives you:

3. *Pray* - Prayer is a two-way conversation with the Lord. Respond from your heart to what he has been revealing to you in his Word, especially taking time to listen to what he may be saying to you personally. You may want to write out your prayer to God and anything he says to you:

4. *Contemplate* — At any time, when you begin to sense the presence of the Lord, stop any mental effort you are making and just rest in and enjoy his presence.

Journal Page

Contemplate Meditate Pray Read Contemplate Meditate Pray Read Contemplate Meditate Pray Read

From St. Cyprian

This may be understood both spiritually and literally, because either way of understanding it is rich in divine usefulness for our salvation. (*Treatise on the Lord's Prayer*, Ch. 18)

From Scripture

Is there anyone among you who, if your child asks for bread, will give a stone? Or if the child asks for a fish, will give a snake? If you then, who are evil, know how to give good gifts to your children, how much more will your Father in heaven give good things to those who ask him! (Matthew 7:9-11)

From The Catechism

The Father who gives us life cannot but give us the nourishment life requires—all appropriate goods and blessings, both material and spiritual. In the Sermon on the Mount, Jesus insists on the filial trust that cooperates with our Father's providence. He is not inviting us to idleness, but wants to relieve us from nagging worry and preoccupation. Such is the filial surrender of the children of God. (CCC: 2830)

Read Pray Meditate Contemplate Read Pray Meditate Contemplate Read Pray Meditate Contemplate

From The Catechism

"Daily" (epiousios) occurs nowhere else in the New Testament. Taken in a temporal sense, this word is a pedagogical repetition of "this day," to confirm us in trust "without reservation." Taken in the qualitative sense, it signifies what is necessary for life, and more broadly every good thing sufficient for subsistence. Taken literally (epi-ousios: "super-essential"), it refers directly to the Bread of Life, the Body of Christ, the "medicine of immortality," without which we have no life within us. (CCC: 2837)

From St. Cyprian

...Christ is the bread of those who are in union with His Body. And we ask that this Bread be given to us daily, that we who are in Christ and daily receive the Eucharist for the food of salvation may not, by the imposition of some heinous sin, be prevented from...partaking of the heavenly Bread and be separated from Christ's Body. (*Treatise on the Lord's Prayer*, Ch 18)

~~~~~~~~~

How is God calling you to act in response to what he has shown you?

And Forgive Us Our Trespasses, As We Forgive

With this petition, the Lord is telling us that guilt can be overcome only by forgiveness, not by retaliation. God is a god who forgives, because he loves his creatures; but forgiveness can only penetrate and become effective in one who is himself forgiving.

"Forgiveness" is a theme that pervades the entire Gospel. We meet it at the very beginning of the Sermon on the Mount in the new interpretation of the fifth commandment, when the Lord says to us: "So if you are offering your gift at the altar, and there remember that your brother has something against you, leave your gift there before the altar and go; first be reconciled to your brother, and then come and offer your gift" (Mt 5:23f.). In so doing, we should keep in mind that God himself—knowing that we human beings stood against him, unreconciled—stepped out of his divinity in order to come toward us, to reconcile us. We should recall that, before giving us the Eucharist, he knelt down before his disciples and washed their dirty feet, cleansing them with his humble love. ...Whatever we have to forgive one another is trivial in comparison with the goodness of God, who forgives us. And ultimately we hear Jesus' petition from the Cross: "Father, forgive them; for they know not what they do" (Lk 23:34).

From *Jesus of Nazareth* by Pope Benedict XVI, p. 157-158.

And Forgive Us Our Trespasses As We Forgive Those Who Trespass Against Us

If we say that we have no sin, we deceive ourselves, and the truth is not in us. If we confess our sins, he who is faithful and just will forgive us our sins and cleanse us from all unrighteousness. *1 John 1:8-9*

In him we have redemption through his blood, the forgiveness of our trespasses, according to the riches of his grace that he lavished on us. *Ephesians 1:7-8a*

Do not judge, so that you may not be judged. For with the judgment you make you will be judged, and the measure you give will be the measure you get. Why do you see the speck in your neighbor's eye, but do not notice the log in your own eye? *Matthew 7:1-3*

As God's chosen ones, holy and beloved, clothe yourselves with compassion, kindness, humility, meekness, and patience. Bear with one another and, if anyone has a complaint against another, forgive each other; just as the Lord has forgiven you, so you also must forgive. Colossians 3:12-13

1. **Read** – Read the verses slowly and prayerfully several times (out loud if possible), savoring the words and letting them sink in. Write down any words or phrases that seem to stand out:

2. **Meditate** – Now begin to think about the words or phrases that stood out to you. Come in faith with the expectation that the Lord will speak to you. Ask him a question such as "What does this mean?" to help you reflect more deeply. You may also think about the passage through the eyes of the author or someone mentioned in the verses. Write down any insights that God gives you:

3. **Pray** – Prayer is a two-way conversation with the Lord. Respond from your heart to what he has been revealing to you in his Word, especially taking time to listen to what he may be saying to you personally. You may want to write out your prayer to God and anything he says to you:

4. **Contemplate** – At any time, when you begin to sense the presence of the Lord, stop any mental effort you are making and just rest in and enjoy his presence.

From St. Cyprian

After this we also entreat for our sins, saying, "And forgive us our debts, as we also forgive our debtors." After the supply of food, pardon of sin is also asked for, that he who is fed by God may live in God, and that not only the present and temporal life may be provided for, but the eternal also, to which we may come if our sins are forgiven. (*The Treatise on the Lord's Prayer*, Ch 22)

Read Pray Meditate Contemplate Read Pray Meditate Contemplate Read Pray Meditate Contemplate Read Pray Meditate Contemplate

From The Catechism

With bold confidence, we began praying to our Father. In begging him that his name be hallowed, we were in fact asking him that we ourselves might be always made more holy. But though we are clothed with the baptismal garment, we do not cease to sin, to turn away from God. Now, in this new petition, we return to him like the prodigal son and, like the tax collector, recognize that we are sinners before him. Our petition begins with a "confession" of our wretchedness and his mercy. Our hope is firm because, in his Son, "we have redemption, the forgiveness of sins." We find the efficacious and undoubted sign of his forgiveness in the sacraments of his Church. (CCC: 2839)

From The Catechism

This petition is astonishing. If it consisted only of the first phrase, "And forgive us our trespasses," it might have been included, implicitly, in the first three petitions of the Lord's Prayer, since Christ's sacrifice is "that sins may be forgiven." But, according to the second phrase, our petition will not be heard unless we have first met a strict requirement. Our petition looks to the future, but our response must come first, for the two parts are joined by the single word "as." (CCC: 2838)

Journal Page

From The Catechism

Now—and this is daunting—this outpouring of mercy cannot penetrate our hearts as long as we have not forgiven those who have trespassed against us. Love, like the Body of Christ, is indivisible; we cannot love the God we cannot see if we do not love the brother or sister we do see. In refusing to forgive our brothers and sisters, our hearts are closed and their hardness makes them impervious to the Father's merciful love; but in confessing our sins, our hearts are opened to his grace. (CCC: 2840)

From St. Cyprian

Therefore also He says in another place, "With what measure you measure, it shall be measured to you again." And the servant who, after having had all his debt forgiven him by his master, would not forgive his fellow-servant, is cast back into prison; because he would not forgive his fellow-servant, he lost the forgiveness that had been shown to himself by his lord. (*The Treatise on the Lord's Prayer*, Ch 23)

Contemplate Meditate Pray Read Contemplate Meditate Pray Read Contemplate Read Pray Meditate Read Pray Meditate

From St. Cyril of Jerusalem

And we make a covenant with God, entreating Him to forgive us our sins, as we also forgive our neighbors their debts. Considering, then, what we receive and what we attain in return, let us not put off, nor delay to forgive one another. The offenses committed against us are slight and trivial, and easily settled; but those which we have committed against God are great and need such mercy as His only is. Take heed, therefore, lest for the slight and trivial sins against you, you shut out for yourself forgiveness from God for your very grievous sins. (*Mystagogical Lecture* 5:16)

Journal Page

~~~~~~~~~

How is God calling you to act in response to what he has shown you?

For we do not have a high priest who is unable to sympathize with our weaknesses, but we have one who in every respect has been tested as we are, yet without sin. (Hebrews 4:15)

The Temptation of Christ by Duccio di Buoninsegna

And Lead Us Not Into Temptation

God certainly does not lead us into temptation. In fact, as Saint James tells us: "Let no one say when he is tempted, 'I am tempted by God'; for God cannot be tempted with evil and he himself tempts no one" (Jas 1:13).

When we pray this, we are saying to God: "I know that I need trials so that my nature can be purified. When you decide to send me these trials, when you give evil some room to maneuver, as you did with Job, then please remember that my strength goes only so far. Don't overestimate my capacity. Don't set too wide the boundaries within which I may be tempted, and be close to me with your protecting hand when it becomes too much for me."

When we pray the sixth petition of the Our Father, we must therefore, on one hand, be ready to take upon ourselves the burden of trials that is meted out to us. On the other hand, the object of the petition is to ask God not to mete out more than we can bear, not to let us slip from his hands.

From *Jesus of Nazareth* by Pope Benedict XVI, p. 160-164.

And Lead Us Not Into Temptation

Then he came to the disciples and found them sleeping; and he said to Peter, "So, could you not stay awake with me one hour? Stay awake and pray that you may not come into the time of trial; the spirit indeed is willing, but the flesh is weak." *Matthew 26:40-41*

So if you think you are standing, watch out that you do not fall. No testing has overtaken you that is not common to everyone. God is faithful, and he will not let you be tested beyond your strength, but with the testing he will also provide the way out so that you may be able to endure it. *1 Corinthians 10:13*

Blessed is anyone who endures temptation. Such a one has stood the test and will receive the crown of life that the Lord has promised to those who love him. No one, when tempted, should say, "I am being tempted by God"; for God cannot be tempted by evil and he himself tempts no one. But one is tempted by one's own desire, being lured and enticed by it; then, when that desire has conceived, it gives birth to sin, and that sin, when it is fully grown, gives birth to death. Do not be deceived, my beloved. *James 1:12-16*

---

1. *Read* – Read the verses slowly and prayerfully several times (out loud if possible), savoring the words and letting them sink in. Write down any words or phrases that seem to stand out:

2. *Meditate* – Now begin to think about the words or phrases that stood out to you. Come in faith with the expectation that the Lord will speak to you. Ask him a question such as "What does this mean?" to help you reflect more deeply. You may also think about the passage through the eyes of the author or someone mentioned in the verses. Write down any insights that God gives you:

3. *Pray* – Prayer is a two-way conversation with the Lord. Respond from your heart to what he has been revealing to you in his Word, especially taking time to listen to what he may be saying to you personally. You may want to write out your prayer to God and anything he says to you:

4. *Contemplate* – At any time, when you begin to sense the presence of the Lord, stop any mental effort you are making and just rest in and enjoy his presence.

Contemplate Meditate Pray Read Contemplate Meditate Pray Read Contemplate Meditate Pray Read Contemplate Meditate Pray Read

From St. Cyprian

When we ask that we may not come into temptation, we are reminded of our infirmity and weakness, lest any should insolently vaunt [brag about] himself, lest any should proudly and arrogantly assume anything to himself, lest any should take to himself the glory either of confession or of suffering as his own, when the Lord Himself, teaching humility, said, "Watch and pray, that ye enter not into temptation; the spirit indeed is willing, but the flesh is weak." (*The Treatise on the Lord's Prayer*, Ch. 26)

From The Catechism

We ask [our Father] not to allow us to take the way that leads to sin. We are engaged in the battle "between flesh and spirit"; this petition implores the Spirit of discernment and strength. (CCC: 2846)

Journal Page

Read   Pray   Meditate   Contemplate   Read   Pray   Meditate   Contemplate   Read   Pray   Meditate   Contemplate   Read   Pray   Meditate   Contemplate

From The Catechism

Such a battle and such a victory become possible only through prayer. It is by his prayer that Jesus vanquishes the tempter, both at the outset of his public mission and in the ultimate struggle of his agony. In this petition to our heavenly Father, Christ unites us to his battle and his agony. He urges us to *vigilance* of the heart in communion with his own. Vigilance is "custody of the heart," and Jesus prayed for us to the Father: "Keep them in your name." The Holy Spirit constantly seeks to awaken us to keep watch. (CCC: 2849)

From St. Cyprian

In (these) words it is shown that the adversary can do nothing against us except God shall have previously permitted it; so that all our fear, and devotion, and obedience may be turned towards God, since in our temptations nothing is permitted to evil unless power is given from Him. (*The Treatise on the Lord's Prayer*, Ch. 25)

~~~~~~~~~

How is God calling you to act in response to what he has shown you?

St. Michael the Archangel,
defend us in battle.
Be our defense against the wickedness and snares of the Devil.
May God rebuke him, we humbly pray,
and do thou,
O Prince of the heavenly hosts,
by the power of God,
thrust into hell Satan,
and all the evil spirits,
who prowl about the world
seeking the ruin of souls. Amen.

But Deliver Us From Evil

The last petition of the Our Father takes up the previous one again and gives it a positive twist. The two petitions are therefore closely connected. In the next-to -last petition the *not* sets the dominant note (do not give the Evil One more room to maneuver than we can bear). In [this] last petition we come before the Father with the hope that is at the center of our faith: "Rescue, redeem, free us!" In the final analysis, it is a plea for redemption.

From *Jesus of Nazareth* by Pope Benedict XVI, p. 164.

But Deliver Us From Evil

For our struggle is not against enemies of blood and flesh, but against the rulers, against the authorities, against the cosmic powers of this present darkness, against the spiritual forces of evil in the heavenly places. *Ephesians 6:11-13*

Jesus said, "Father,... "I am not asking you to take them out of the world, but I ask you to protect them from the evil one. They do not belong to the world, just as I do not belong to the world." *John 17:15-16*

Grace to you and peace from God our Father and the Lord Jesus Christ, who gave himself for our sins to set us free from the present evil age, according to the will of our God and Father, to whom be the glory forever and ever. Amen. *Galatians 1:4*

But the Lord is faithful; he will strengthen you and guard you from the evil one. *2 Thessalonians 3:3*

---

1. *Read* — Read the verses slowly and prayerfully several times (out loud if possible), savoring the words and letting them sink in. Write down any words or phrases that seem to stand out:

2. *Meditate* – Now begin to think about the words or phrases that stood out to you. Come in faith with the expectation that the Lord will speak to you. Ask him a question such as "What does this mean?" to help you reflect more deeply. You may also think about the passage through the eyes of the author or someone mentioned in the verses. Write down any insights that God gives you:

3. *Pray* – Prayer is a two-way conversation with the Lord. Respond from your heart to what he has been revealing to you in his Word, especially taking time to listen to what he may be saying to you personally. You may want to write out your prayer to God and anything he says to you:

4. *Contemplate* — At any time, when you begin to sense the presence of the Lord, stop any mental effort you are making and just rest in and enjoy his presence.

From The Catechism

The last petition to our Father is also included in Jesus' prayer: "I am not asking you to take them out of the world, but I ask you to protect them from the evil one." ...In this petition, evil is not an abstraction, but refers to a person, Satan, the Evil One, the angel who opposes God.
(CCC: 2850-2851)

Read Pray Meditate Contemplate Read Pray Meditate Contemplate Read Pray Meditate Contemplate Read Pray Meditate Contemplate

From St. Ambrose

The Lord who has taken away your sin and pardoned your faults also protects you and keeps you from the wiles of your adversary the devil, so that the enemy, who is accustomed to leading into sin, may not surprise you. One who entrusts himself to God does not dread the devil. "If God is for us, who is against us?" *On the Sacraments*, Book V, Ch 4:30.

From The Catechism

When we ask to be delivered from the Evil One, we pray as well to be freed from all evils, present, past, and future, of which he is the author or instigator. In this final petition, the Church brings before the Father all the distress of the world. Along with deliverance from the evils that overwhelm humanity, she implores the precious gift of peace and the grace of perseverance in expectation of Christ's return. (CCC: 2854)

Journal Page

Read Pray Meditate Contemplate Read Pray Meditate Contemplate Read Pray Meditate Contemplate Read Pray Meditate Contemplate

From The Roman Missal

Deliver us, Lord, we beseech you, from every evil and grant us peace in our day, so that aided by your mercy we might be ever free from sin and protected from all anxiety, as we await the blessed hope and the coming of our Savior, Jesus Christ. (Roman Missal, Embolism after the Lord's Prayer; CCC: 2854.)

From St. Cyprian
And when we say, Deliver us from evil, there remains nothing further which ought to be asked. When we have once asked for God's protection against evil, and have obtained it, then against everything which the devil and the world work against us we stand secure and safe. For what fear is there in this life, to the man whose guardian in this life is God? (From *The Treatise on the Lord's Prayer*, Ch. 27)

~~~~~~~~~

How is God calling you to act in response to what he has shown you?

The Doxology

For The Kingdom And The Power And The Glory Are Yours Now And Forever, Amen.

Although the words of the doxology are not found in the earliest manuscripts of the New Testament, they can be found in the ancient liturgies of the Church. The *Didache* (an early church training manual called the "The Teaching of the Twelve Apostles," written between 50-100 AD) includes the doxology in the section containing instructions on church practice and order (*Didache* 8:2).

The Doxology provides for us the all-pervading, undergirding reason that we dare to pray The Our Father. In the liturgy of the Mass, after the Priest prays, "Deliver us, Lord, we pray, from every evil..." we raise our voices together to proclaim that very reason: "For [because] the kingdom and the power and the glory are yours now and forever, Amen."

Thus we are able pray with confidence and certain hope because we are God's children and we know that He is our holy Father who is both powerful and loving (Ps 62:11), and that His Kingdom is present now and always.

For The Kingdom And The Power And The Glory Are Yours Now And Forever, Amen

Then I heard every creature in heaven and on earth and under the earth and in the sea, and all that is in them, singing, "To the one seated on the throne and to the Lamb be blessing and honor and glory and might forever and ever!" And the four living creatures said, "Amen!" And the elders fell down and worshiped. *Revelation 5:13-14*

Now to him who by the power at work within us is able to accomplish abundantly far more than all we can ask or imagine, to him be glory in the church and in Christ Jesus to all generations, forever and ever. Amen. *Ephesians 3:20-21*

To the King of the ages, immortal, invisible, the only God, be honor and glory forever and ever. Amen. *1 Timothy 1:17*

---

1. *Read* — Read the verses slowly and prayerfully several times (out loud if possible), savoring the words and letting them sink in. Write down any words or phrases that seem to stand out:

2. *Meditate* - Now begin to think about the words or phrases that stood out to you. Come in faith with the expectation that the Lord will speak to you. Ask him a question such as "What does this mean?" to help you reflect more deeply. You may also think about the passage through the eyes of the author or someone mentioned in the verses. Write down any insights that God gives you:

3. *Pray* - Prayer is a two-way conversation with the Lord. Respond from your heart to what he has been revealing to you in his Word, especially taking time to listen to what he may be saying to you personally. You may want to write out your prayer to God and anything he says to you:

4. *Contemplate* — At any time, when you begin to sense the presence of the Lord, stop any mental effort you are making and just rest in and enjoy his presence.

Journal Page

From St. John Chrysostom

Having then made us prepared for conflict by recalling to our minds the Enemy, and having cut away from us all our negligence, He again encourages us and raises our spirits by bringing to our remembrance the King under whom we are arrayed and by describing Him as more powerful than all, "For thine," He says, "is the kingdom and the power and the glory." (*Homily XIX on The Gospel of Matthew*)

Contemplate Meditate Pray Read Contemplate Meditate Pray Read Contemplate Meditate Pray Read

From The Catechism

The final doxology, "For the kingdom, the power and the glory are yours, now and forever," takes up again, by inclusion, the first three petitions to our Father: the glorification of his name, the coming of his reign, and the power of his saving will. But these prayers are now proclaimed as adoration and thanksgiving, as in the liturgy of heaven. The ruler of this world has mendaciously [deceitfully] attributed to himself the three titles of kingship, power, and glory. Christ, the Lord, restores them to his Father and our Father, until he hands over the kingdom to him when the mystery of salvation will be brought to its completion and God will be all in all. (CCC: 2855)

Journal Page

Read Pray Meditate Contemplate Read Pray Meditate Contemplate Read Pray Meditate Contemplate

~~~~~~~~~

How is God calling you to act in response to what he has shown you?

Then David blessed the LORD in the presence of
all the assembly;

David said: "Blessed are you, O LORD,

the God of our ancestor Israel,

forever and ever.

Yours, O LORD, are the greatness, the power,

the glory, the victory, and the majesty;

for all that is in the heavens

and on the earth is yours;

yours is the kingdom, O LORD,

and you are exalted as head above all.

Riches and honor come from you,

and you rule over all.

In your hand are power and might;

and it is in your hand to make great

and to give strength to all.

And now, our God,

we give thanks to you

and praise your glorious name.

1 Chronicles 29:10-13

Notes

Page 5. Francis. *Letter of Pope Francis to the Carmelites on the Occasion of General Chapter 2013*. http://www.carmelites.net/news/letter-of-pope-francis-to-the-carmelites-on-the-occasion-of-general-chapter-2013/ (accessed January 20, 2014).

Page 8, 9. *The Catechism of the Catholic Church*, 2nd Edition. Libreria Editrice Vaticana, Citta del Vaticano. 1994, 1997.

Page 7. Ratzinger, Joseph, Pope Benedict XVI. *Jesus of Nazareth*. Translated by Adrian J. Walker. New York: Doubleday, 2007, 132.

Page 7. St. Cyprian. *Treatise IV, On the Lord's Prayer*. Ch. 3. http://www.ccel.org/ccel/schaff/anf05.iv.v.iv.html (accessed December 18, 2013).

Page 11. John Paul II. *Apostolic Letter, Novo Millennio Ineunte, to the Bishops Clergy and Lay Faithful at the Close of the Great Jubilee of the Year 2000*, 39. http://www.vatican.va/holy_father/john_paul_ii/apost_letters/documents/hf_jp-ii_apl_20010106_novo-millennio-ineunte_en.html (accessed December 18, 2013).

Page 12. Synod of Bishops XII Ordinary General Assembly 2007. *The Word of God in the Life and Mission of the Church*. http://www.vatican.va/roman_curia/synod/documents/rc_synod_doc_20070427_lineamenta-xii-assembly_en.html (accessed January 20, 2014).

Page 13. Benedict XVI. *Address of His Holiness Benedict XVI to the Participants in the International Congress Organized to Commemorate the 40th Anniversary of the Dogmatic Constitution on Divine Revelation "Die Verbum."* Castel Gandolfo, Friday, 16 September 2005. http://www.vatican.va/holy_father/benedict_xvi/speeches/2005/september/documents/hf_ben-xvi_spe_20050916_40-dei-verbum_en.html (accessed December 18, 2013).

Page 13. Benedict XVI. *Post-Synodal Apostolic Exhortation, Verbum Domini, of the Holy Father Benedict XVI to the Bishops, Clergy, Consecrated Persons and the Lay Faithful on the Word of God in the Life and Mission of the Church*. 86. October 2008. http://www.vatican.va/holy_father/benedict_xvi/apost_exhortations/documents/hf_ben-xvi_exh_20100930_verbum-domini_en.html (accessed December 16, 2013).

Page 16. Caussade, Jean-Pierre de. *Abandonment to Divine Providence*. 1921. Reprint, Kessinger Publishing, n.d., 13.

Page 17. Sam Anthony Morello, OCD *Lectio Divina And the Practice of Teresian Prayer*, .Spiritual Life Summer 1991. Washington Province of Discalced Carmelites, ICS Publications. 22.

Page 18. Casey, Michael. *Sacred Reading: The Ancient Art of Lectio Divina*. Liguori, MO: Triumph Books, 1996, 61.

Page 18. Hall, Thelma. *Too Deep For Words: Rediscovering Lectio Divina*. New York: Paulist Pr, 1988, 44.

Page 19. Benedict XVI. *Message to the People of God of the XII Ordinary Assembly of the Synod of Bishops: Conclusion*, October 27, 2008. http://www.vatican.va/roman_curia/synod/documents/rc_synod_doc_20081024_message-synod_en.html (accessed September 17, 2011.).

Page 19. St. John of the Cross, *Dark Night of the Soul*. Translated by E. Allison Peers. New York: Image Books, 1959, 72.

Page 20. Gildas, M. *St. Bernard of Clairvaux*. The Catholic Encyclopedia. New York: Robert Appleton Company. http://www.newadvent.org/cathen/02498d.htm (accessed December 8, 2013).

Page 21. Pennington, M. Basil. *Lectio Divina: Renewing the Ancient Practice of Praying the Scriptures*. New York: The Crossroad Publishing Company, 1998, 90.

Page 21. Augustine. *The Confessions*. Translated and edited by Philip Burton. New York: Alfred A. Knopf, Everyman's Library, 2001, 48.

Page 21. Guigo II, *The Ladder of Monks: A Letter On the Contemplative Life and Twelve Meditations*. trans. Edmund Colledge and James Walsh. Kalamazoo, MI: Cistercian Publications, 1979, 74.

Page 21. Benedict XVI. *Verbum Domini*. 85.

Pages 29, 37, 45,53,59, 67, 75, 85, 93. Ratzinger, Joseph, Pope Benedict XVI. *Jesus of Nazareth*. Translated by Adrian J. Walker. New York: Doubleday, 2007.

Pages 31-105. *The Catechism of the Catholic Church*, 2nd Edition. Libreria Editrice Vaticana, Citta del Vaticano. 1994, 1997. Various.

Page 34, 42, 49, 57, 63, 64, 70, 73, 77, 81, 88, 91, 99. St. Cyprian. *Treatise IV, On the Lord's Prayer*. http://www.ccel.org/ccel/schaff/anf05.iv.v.iv.html (accessed December 18, 2013).

Page 56. St. Augustine of Hippo. *On the Sermon on the Mount*: *Extended Annotated Edition*. eBook, Jazzybee Verlag, 2012.

Page 41, 47, 103. St. John Chrysostom. Homily 19 on Matthew, 6. http://www.newadvent.org/fathers/200119.htm (accessed December 18, 2013).

Page 82. St. Cyril of Jerusalem. *The Catechetical and Mystagogical Lectures of St. Cyril of Jerusalem*. e-book by David Nicoll, 2012. *Mystagogical Lecture* 5:16.

Page 96. St. Ambrose. *On the Mysteries and the Treatise on the Sacraments*. Trans. T. Thompson. New York: Macmillan Co, 1919, 128. https://archive.org/stream/stambroseonmyste00ambr#page/128/mode/2up (accessed December 19, 2013).

Page 101. Holmes, Michael W., editor. *The Apostolic Fathers in English*. Grand Rapids, MI: Baker Academic, 2006, 167.

The author initially developed the *Introduction to Lectio Divina*, the *Lectio Divina Summary* and the descriptions of the four stages of *lectio divina* for her research project for her doctoral thesis, *Lectio Divina as a Catalyst for Spiritual Growth: A Case Study Among Mature Believers,* © 2012. She also has incorporated these in similar form in several other prayer guides, including the *Lectio Divina Prayer Guides* for Communities of Prayer, © 2011, 2012 and Scripture-based Reflective Prayer Guides, © 2010-2013.

Additional Source

Johnson, Katherine Mills. *Lectio Divina as a Catalyst for Spiritual Growth: A Case Study Among Mature Believers*. Doctor of Ministry Thesis, Gordon-Conwell Theological Seminary, 2012.

Photo Credits

Page 52, 55, 58, 61, 72, 92, 95. Fr. Lawrence Lew, used by permission.

Page 12. Taken by author.

Page 4, 14, 16, 18, 21, 24, 44. Shutterstock.com.

All other illustrations are in the public domain to the best knowledge of the author.

Made in the USA
Las Vegas, NV
12 August 2021